Contents

Some words are printed in bold, **like this**. You can find out what they mean on page 30. You can also look in the box at the bottom of the page where they first appear.

In the beginning

We start this tale nearly 300 million years ago. Our setting is a warm, shallow ocean. It is prehistoric times. Prehistoric means a very long time ago.

We begin on the ocean floor with a **sponge**. A sponge is a simple animal. For a few years, this sponge lives in the ocean. But we are not going to look at its short life in the ocean. We are going to look at what happens to this sponge over millions of years.

It will travel around Earth. It will go through many changes. It will go through the **rock cycle** as it changes from one form to another.

Sponge fact

There are different types of sponge. The barrel sponge can grow so large that a person can fit inside one!

rock cycle   process in which rock changes from one form to another

Tales of a Prehistoric Sponge

Clay Cryute

Raintree

www.raintreepublishers.co.uk

Visit our website to find out more information about **Raintree** books.

To order:
☎ Phone 44 (0) 1865 888112
📄 Send a fax to 44 (0) 1865 314091
💻 Visit the Raintree bookshop at **www.raintreepublishers.co.uk** to browse our catalogue and order online.

First published in Great Britain by Raintree, Halley Court, Jordan Hill, Oxford OX2 8EJ, part of Harcourt Education.
Raintree is a registered trademark of Harcourt Education Ltd.

Editorial: Lucy Thunder and Richard Woodham
Design: Michelle Lisseter, Carolyn Gibson, and Bigtop
Illustrations: Darren Lingard
Picture Research: Melissa Allison and Fiona Orbell
Production: Camilla Crask

Originated by Dot Gradations Ltd
Printed and bound in Italy by Printer Trento srl

ISBN 1 844 43155 X (hardback)
10 09 08 07 06
10 9 8 7 6 5 4 3 2 1

ISBN 1 844 43254 8 (paperback)
11 10 09 08 07
10 9 8 7 6 5 4 3 2 1

British Library Cataloguing in Publication Data
Cryute, Clay
Tales of a Prehistoric Sponge: The rock cycle
551.9
A full catalogue record for this book is available from the British Library.

Acknowledgements

The publishers would like to thank the following for permission to reproduce photographs: AKG Images p. 22–23; Alamy p. 29 (lower) (Leslie Garland Picture Library); Corbis pp. 4 (Robert Yin), 5 (both) (Jonathan Blair), 8–9 (DK Images), 10–11 (Ecoscene/Chinch Gryniewicz), 17 (lower) (James L. Amos), 18–19 (John Noble), 20–21 (Larry Neubauer), 29 (top) (DK Images); Geoscience Features p. 28; Getty Images p. 13 inset (Stockdisc Classic); Getty p. 26–27 (Photographers Choice); Photolibrary.com p. 17 (top) (Index Stock); Science Photo Library pp. 6–7 (Louise K. Broman), 12–13 (Dr. Juerg Alaen), 24 (inset) (Adam Hart-Davis), 24–25 (NASA).

Cover photograph of a Caribbean coral reef, reproduced with permission of Corbis (Stephen Frink).

The publishers would like to thank Nancy Harris and Harold Pratt for their assistance in the preparation of this book.

Every effort has been made to contact copyright holders of any material reproduced in this book. Any omissions will be rectified in subsequent printings if notice is given to the publishers.

The paper used to print this book comes from sustainable resources.

▼We begin in a warm, shallow ocean nearly 300 million years ago.

sponge

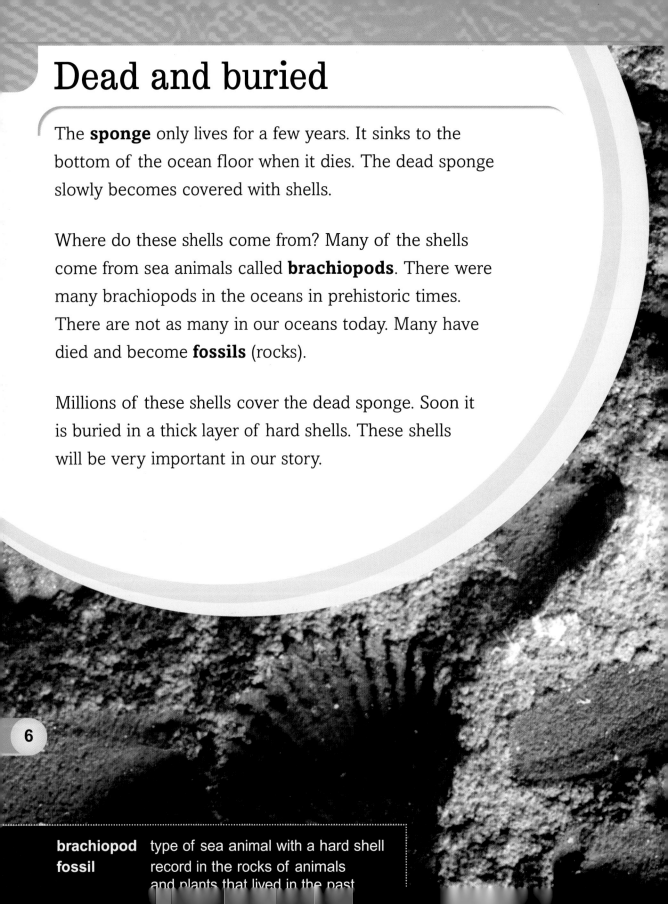

Dead and buried

The **sponge** only lives for a few years. It sinks to the bottom of the ocean floor when it dies. The dead sponge slowly becomes covered with shells.

Where do these shells come from? Many of the shells come from sea animals called **brachiopods**. There were many brachiopods in the oceans in prehistoric times. There are not as many in our oceans today. Many have died and become **fossils** (rocks).

Millions of these shells cover the dead sponge. Soon it is buried in a thick layer of hard shells. These shells will be very important in our story.

brachiopod   type of sea animal with a hard shell
fossil   record in the rocks of animals
                       and plants that lived in the past

Fossils

You can still see the shapes of brachiopods that died millions of years ago. The soft parts of their bodies have rotted away. But their shells have hardened and turned to rock. They have become fossils.

7

These cliffs are ▼
made of limestone.

Harder times

More and more shells pile up on top of the dead **sponge**. Then a change begins to happen. The soft parts of the sponge's body rot away. The sponge's body very slowly turns to rock. The sponge becomes a **fossil**.

The layers of shells are also changing. They are squeezed and squashed. The shells are broken into small pieces. These pieces of shell are a type of **sediment**.

The layers of sediment are squeezed together. They form **sedimentary rock**. The sponge fossil is now part of this sedimentary rock. The rock is called limestone.

Limestone

Limestone is a sedimentary rock. It is made from the shells of dead sea animals. You can often find fossils in limestone.

sediment   material such as mud, sand, gravel, or bits of shells
sedimentary rock   rock formed from layers of material squeezed together

Getting pushed around

The limestone sits for thousands of years. It gets buried deeper and deeper. There are more layers of **sedimentary rock** above and below it.

Earth's surface has many sections. These sections are called **plates**. The limestone layers are part of a plate. Underneath the plates is a thick layer of rock. This layer is called the **mantle**. The rocks in the mantle are soft and almost melted.

The plates move on top of the mantle. Some plates push against each other.

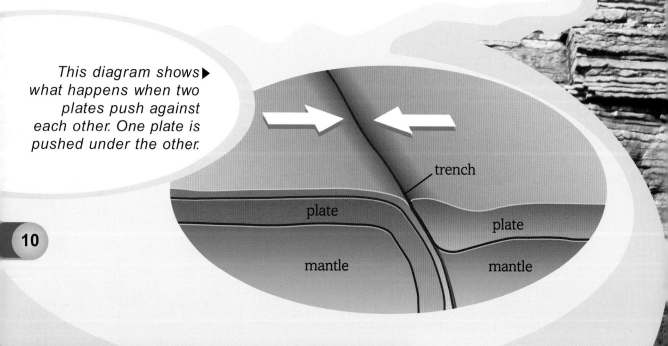

This diagram shows ▶ what happens when two plates push against each other. One plate is pushed under the other.

trench

plate

plate

mantle

mantle

mantle   thick layer of soft and almost-melted rock
plate   large section of the Earth's surface

▼ Sedimentary rock forms in layers. You can see the layers in this photo.

11

This volcano is ▼
erupting. Magma is
being forced out of it.

Hot rock

One **plate** is slowly bent when it is pushed. Cracks form in this plate. Melted rock starts to push up through some of the cracks. This melted rock is called **magma**.

The magma pours out of a volcano. After a volcano erupts, the melted rock slowly cools down. It forms a new type of rock. Rocks that are formed when melted rock cools down are called **igneous rocks**.

But where is the limestone, which was once a **sponge**?

Igneous rocks

This rock is called pumice. Pumice is an igneous rock. It forms when melted rock from a volcano cools down and hardens.

13

igneous rock   rock that is formed when melted rock cools and hardens

Big changes

Slowly the limestone rock is pushed deeper underground. Cracks and holes form in the thick layer of rock. These cracks begin to fill up with hot **magma** (melted rock).

The limestone is changing. Two things cause it to change. First, the layers of rock above the limestone press down on it. The limestone is under pressure. Second, the limestone is heated by the magma.

The limestone changes into a **metamorphic rock**. This happens because the limestone has been heated under pressure.

The sedimentary rock is ▶ pushed underground towards the hot mantle. The heat and pressure change the sedimentary rock into a metamorphic rock.

metamorphic rock   rock that forms when sedimentary or igneous

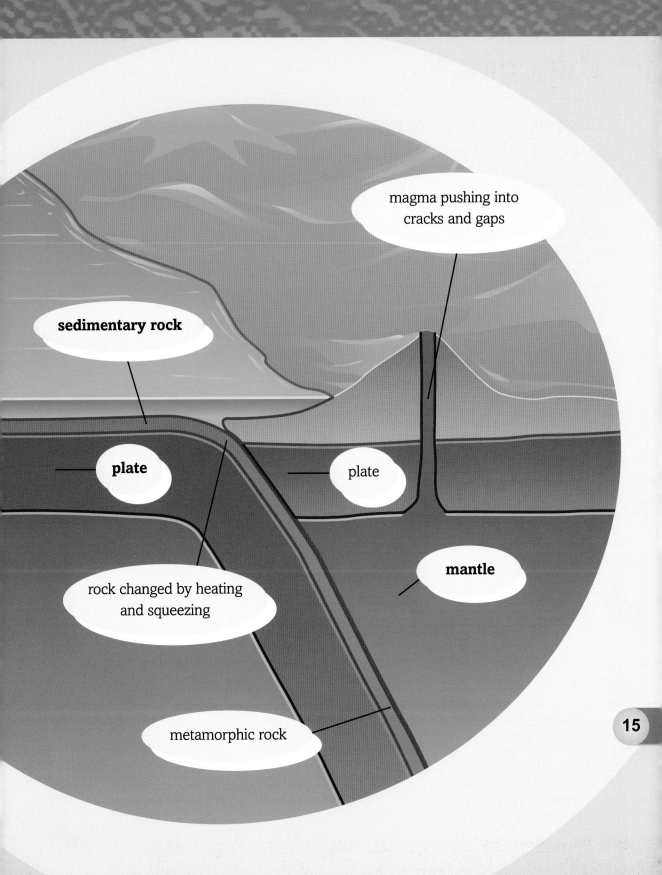

magma pushing into cracks and gaps

sedimentary rock

plate

plate

rock changed by heating and squeezing

mantle

metamorphic rock

Making marble

The change from limestone to **metamorphic rock** takes a very long time. It is thousands of years before the melted rock cools down. Heat and pressure have turned the limestone into a harder, smoother rock. It becomes a type of metamorphic rock called marble.

The marble is still part of the **plate**. The plate has continued to move and change. It is now a long way from the ocean where the **sponge** lived. It now has folds that make a small group of hills.

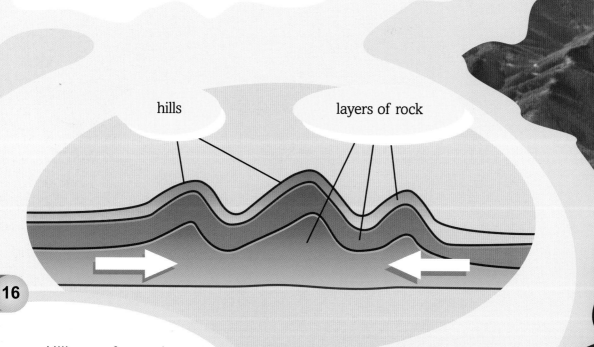

hills

layers of rock

Hills can form when ▲ the ends of a plate are pushed together. The rocks in the plate rise up and form hills.

◀ Marble can be found in many different colours.

17

▲ Folds in the rock have formed this small group of hills.

Water power

The marble stays deep in the hills for millions of years. Not much happens to the rock. But a lot happens around it. A river begins to flow between the hills. The water wears down and breaks apart some of the rocks. The moving water then carries away the pieces of rock. This process is called **erosion**.

The moving water acts like sandpaper. It wears away the hills. A valley forms. The marble is still in the hills. It gets closer to the surface as the river wears away more rock.

Soil fact

Soil is made from the wearing away of rocks. Rocks are slowly broken down into tiny pieces. These tiny pieces become soil. It can take up to 1,000 years to form one pinch of soil!

erosion   movement of small pieces of rock from one place to another

▼ Over thousands of years a river cut a deep valley between these hills.

valley

glacier

V-shaped valley

river

For thousands of years, ▲ ice sheets and glaciers covered many northern parts of the world.

Moving along

The river continues to flow for thousands of years. It slowly wears away at the hills. Then Earth's weather changes in a big way. It gets very cold. It stays that way, on and off, until about 11,000 years ago. This time of cold weather is known as the Ice Age.

The valley fills with snow. The snow becomes a **glacier**. The icy glacier moves slowly downhill. The glacier causes **erosion**. It takes rocks from the ground with it.

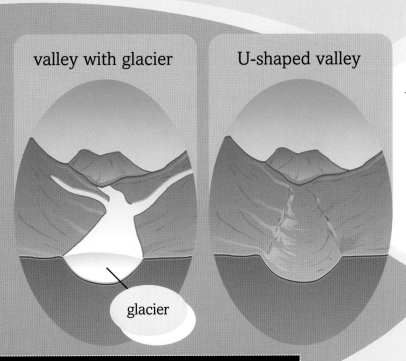

valley with glacier

U-shaped valley

glacier

◀ *A fast-flowing river cuts a V-shaped valley. But a glacier wears away the sides and the bottom of a valley. A glacier leaves a U-shaped valley when it melts.*

glacier   huge sheet of slow-moving ice

Carved into a statue

The marble survives the Ice Age. It stays in the hillside for many years. It might have stayed there for a million years, but . . .

People begin digging the marble out of the hills. They use the marble on buildings to make them beautiful. An artist carves the marble into a statue.

It has been a long journey for this **sponge**. It began millions of years ago in the ocean.

This statue has been carved▶ from a block of marble.

Wearing away

The marble statue decorates a building for hundreds of years. Wind and rain slowly wear away the rock. They cause small pieces to break off. The small pieces are washed away. This process is called **erosion**. The small pieces of marble become **sediment**.

The sediment flows down a drain. The drain leads to a river. The river carries the sediment to the ocean. Then the sediment falls to the ocean floor. This process is called **deposition**.

The disappearing statue

Eventually, a stone statue will be worn away by erosion. Small pieces of stone are slowly broken off. They are then carried away. At last, the stone statue disappears!

deposition   when sediment is dropped in a place

▲This photo shows the place where a river meets the ocean. The light blue parts show where sediment is flowing out from the river into the sea.

Back in the water

After nearly 300 million years we are back at the bottom of the ocean. But this is not the end of the story. More soil and pieces of rock flow into the ocean every day. This **sediment** falls to the ocean floor. The layers of sediment build up. They eventually become new **sedimentary rock**.

The **rock cycle** that changed the **sponge** over millions of years will continue. The rock will never become a living sponge again. But it can change into different sedimentary, **igneous**, and **metamorphic rocks**. If you can wait a few thousand years, you might just learn what type of rock it becomes next!

This is a type of sponge ▶ that can be found in the ocean today. In a few million years, it may become part of a sedimentary rock.

The rock cycle

The way that rocks can change over time is known as the **rock cycle**. The story of the prehistoric sponge is just one of many forms of the rock cycle.

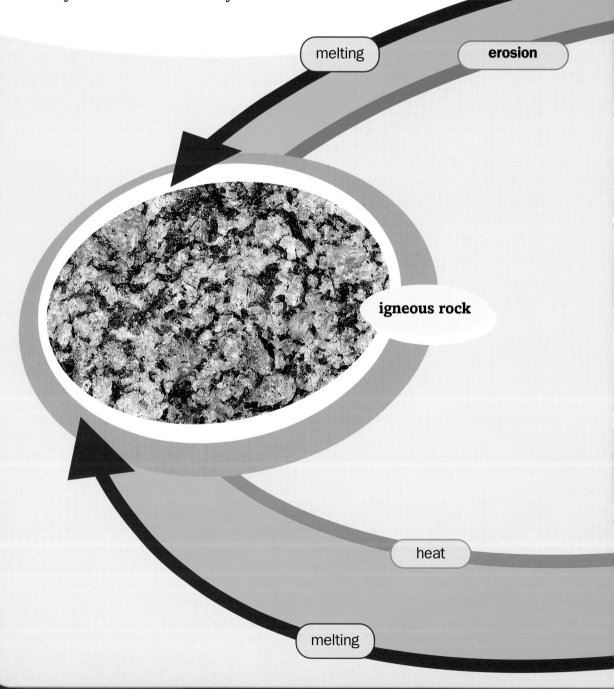

melting

erosion

igneous rock

heat

melting

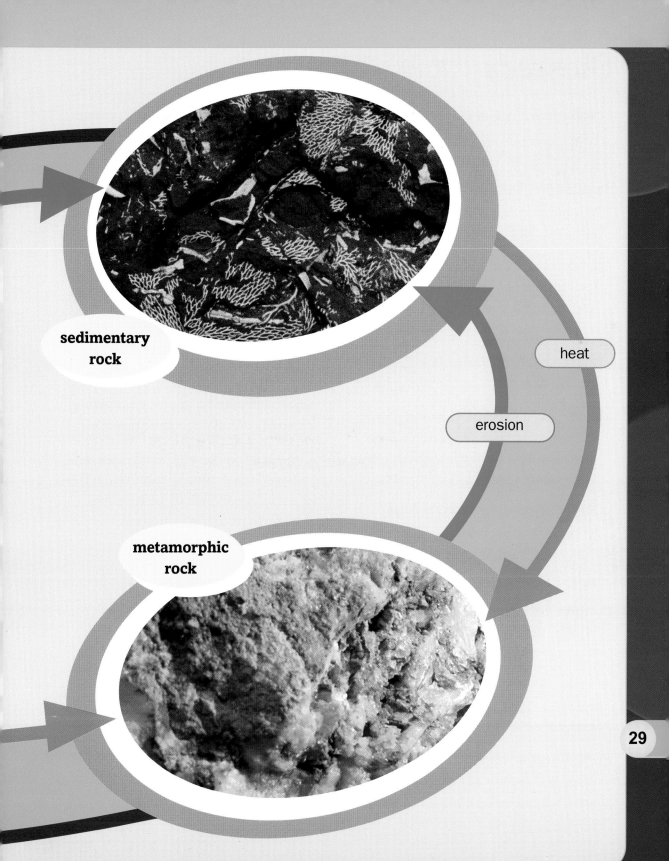

sedimentary
rock

heat

erosion

metamorphic
rock

Glossary

brachiopod type of sea animal with a hard shell. Their fossil shells can be found in limestone.

deposition when sediment is dropped in a place. The sediment eventually turns into sedimentary rock.

erosion movement of small pieces of rock from one place to another. Wind and water often erode pieces of rock.

fossil record in rocks of animals and plants that lived in the past. Fossils are often found in sedimentary rocks.

glacier huge sheet of slow-moving ice. Glaciers wear away the valleys that they flow through, making them deeper and wider.

igneous rock rock that is formed when melted rock cools and hardens. Pumice and granite are types of igneous rock.

magma melted rock deep underground. Magma can cool to form igneous rocks such as granite.

mantle thick layer of soft and almost-melted rock. The mantle is found just under the Earth's surface.

metamorphic rock rock that forms when sedimentary or igneous rocks are changed by heat and pressure. Marble is a metamorphic rock.

plate large section of Earth's surface. The whole of Earth's surface is broken into several plates.

rock cycle process in which rock changes from one form to another. For example, sedimentary rocks can become metamorphic rocks if they are heated and squashed.

sediment material such as mud, sand, gravel, or bits of shells. Mud, sand, and grit are all sediments.

sedimentary rock rock formed from layers of material squeezed together. Limestone and sandstone are both sedimentary rocks.

sponge simple animal that lives in the ocean. Some kinds of bath sponge are made from these animals.

Want to know more?

Books

- *Rock and Fossil Hunter*, Ben Morgan (Dorling Kindersley, 2005)
- *Rocks and Fossils*, Chris Pellant (Kingfisher, 2003).
- *Supercroc*, Chris Sloan (National Geographic Books, 2002)
- *The Rock Cycle*, Melanie Ostopowich (Weigl, 2004)
- *The Pebble in My Pocket*, Meredith Hooper (Frances Lincoln, 1997).

Websites

- www.oum.ox.ac.uk/children/kidscoll.htm
  Oxford University Museum website has an enjoyable section on the rock cycle.
- ology.amnh.org/earth/index.html
  Ology is the American Museum of Natural History's website for young people. This is the section on Earth and rocks.

If you want to know how rocks are shaped in weird and wonderful ways, read ***The Disappearing Mountain and Other Earth Mysteries***.

If you want to learn more about fossils, read ***Journal of a Fossil Hunter***.

Index